THE
DIGESTIVE SYSTEM

How Living Creatures Use Food

Also by the authors:

In preparation:
  The Muscular System:
    How Living Creatures Move

THE
DIGESTIVE SYSTEM
How Living Creatures Use Food

by
Dr. Alvin Silverstein
and Virginia B. Silverstein

Illustrated by Mel Erikson

PRENTICE-HALL, INC.
Englewood Cliffs, N.J.

THE DIGESTIVE SYSTEM: *How Living Creatures Use Food*
by Dr. Alvin Silverstein and Virginia B. Silverstein

13–213009–2

Library of Congress Catalog Card Number: 75–102279

Printed in the United States of America • *J*

Prentice-Hall International, Inc., London
Prentice-Hall of Australia, Pty. Ltd., Sydney
Prentice-Hall of Canada, Ltd., Toronto
Prentice-Hall of India Private Ltd., New Delhi
Prentice-Hall of Japan, Inc., Tokyo

Third printing. . . . . October, 1971

CONTENTS

For Elizabeth Stevenson

1

Digestion in the Living World

What is your favorite food? A strawberry ice-cream sundae? A thick juicy steak? An apple pie fresh out of the oven?

Just thinking about these tasty foods, you may find that your mouth is beginning to water. This is the first step in a long series of processes that the body uses to break down the foods we eat. From them we get energy and new building materials. This process of breaking down foods into smaller bits that can be used by the body is called *digestion*.

All the living things of the world must digest their food before they can use it. The tiniest fleas and the largest whales, the invisible bacteria that swarm about us, and the plants of the forests and fields and the sea—all these must digest their food.

You might wonder why living things have to digest foods. Why can't they just use them as they are taken into the body? There are a number of reasons.

One of these reasons is size. You can see this for yourself. Take a bite-sized piece of cheese or bread, and with a knife, cut it in half. Then cut it again and again and again, until it is so small that you cannot cut it anymore. The pieces of cheese or bread are now just small crumbs. But you can make them even smaller if you cut and scrape at them with the points of two pins. Finally the crumbs are so small that you can hardly see them. If you put one on the head of one of the pins, it would be just a tiny speck.

Yet even this little speck of food is many times larger than a human cell. The cells of our bodies are so small that we cannot see them without a microscope. And so the food would have to be broken down into much smaller pieces before it would be able to pass *into* a cell, where it will be used. These pieces would have to be much smaller than the cell itself.

Size is not the only reason that food must be broken down before it can be used by the body. Food is made up of various kinds of chemicals, and often these substances are not exactly the same as the chemicals of the body. So when food is to be used as building materials, the body must break down or digest these substances into smaller building blocks; only then can it build them up into the right kinds of larger chemicals that it needs.

For example, each time you eat meat or cheese, or most other kinds of foods, you are taking into your body many different kinds of proteins. These proteins are very large chemicals. Each is made up of as many as hundreds or even thousands of smaller building blocks called *amino acids*. You might think of a protein as a long string of colored beads. Each color represents a different kind of amino acid. And the pattern that the different colors make on the string is different for each kind of protein. In your body there are thousands of different patterns. Some scientists think that there may be more than a hundred thousand different kinds of proteins in the human body. Humans have their own special kinds of proteins. So do other animals. Cows have their own set of proteins, as do fishes and plants.

So when we eat a piece of steak, we are taking in cow proteins. Our body breaks them down into amino acids, and then later uses these acids to build up into human proteins.

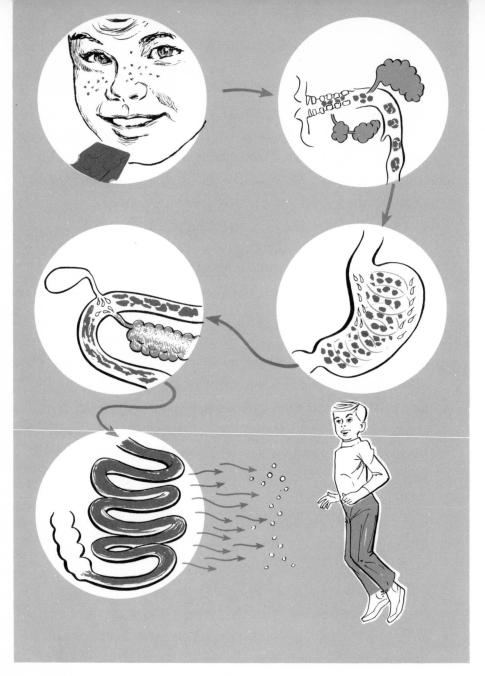

The food that we eat is digested into simpler chemicals that are used by the body for energy and building materials.

Some of the small chemicals that are found when larger bits of food are digested are not used as building blocks in the body. Instead, they are broken down even further to release the energy that is bound up within them. This energy is very important for living things. It provides the power for everything they do, from all kinds of chemical reactions that take place inside the cells themselves to activities of the whole body, such as running and jumping and swimming.

To get the energy and building materials that they need in order to live, animals and plants must have food. Some make their own, while others must get food by eating other living things. There are many ways in which this is done.

2

How Living Things Get Their Food

The world is filled with animals and plants of many different sizes and shapes and habits. Some animals swim in the deep seas; others crawl or hop or run on the land, over the deserts, through grassy meadows, and among the trees of the forests. Some plants are so small that they cannot be seen without a microscope, while others tower hundreds of feet into the air. Yet all these living things must have foods to use for energy and new building materials as they live and grow.

Plants do not have to eat as we and other animals do. They make enough food for their own needs. They take in very simple chemicals—a gas called carbon dioxide from the air and water from the soil or sea or pond in which they live. Then, using the energy from sunlight, they bind these simple chemicals together into larger, more complicated chemicals. Some of these are stored away to be used later as food materials.

Animals cannot make their own food. They must take in food chemicals that have already been made by other living things. Many animals eat plants. Some insects, such as aphids or plant lice, have a long, thin sucking tube. With it they pierce the leaf or stem or root of a plant and suck its juices. Other insects, such as beetles of various kinds, chew pieces of leaves. Larger animals also eat plants. Mice nibble on seeds, and rabbits and cows graze on tender greens. Animals that eat only plants are called *herbivorous* (her-BIV-or-us) *animals*, from words meaning "grass-eating."

Some animals would starve to death if all they had to eat were plants. They eat mainly other animals and are called *carnivorous* (car-NIV-or-us) *animals*, from words meaning "meat-eating." Lions and tigers, foxes and wolves, pounce upon their prey and gorge themselves. Seals catch fish, and indeed, many larger fish gobble up smaller fish, which eat smaller fish still. Even some insects, such as praying mantises and giant water beetles, kill and eat other animals.

But, you might be wondering, where do *we* fit in? Humans do not eat only plants or only meat. And there are other animals also, such as pigs and rats,

Herbivores eat mainly plant food; carnivores eat meat; omnivores can eat anything.

that eat both meat and plants. These are *omnivorous* (om-NIV-or-us) *animals*, so called from words meaning "eating everything."

With all the different kinds of creatures on the earth and the varied things they eat, it is surprising how similar they are in the ways they digest their food. Although their digestive systems often look very different from one another, they work in much the same way to break down large chemicals into smaller building blocks. Let us find out more about how our own digestive system works so that we can compare it with the processes of digestion in other living things.

8

3

Our Digestive System

In your body there is a tube, running from one end to the other. It is not a straight tube; it twists and turns and coils about. It bulges in some places and is pinched in at others. This tube is your *digestive tract*. Your "inner tube" may be as much as twenty feet long! Indeed, the digestive tract of an adult man may be thirty feet long or more.

How could such a long tube fit into you? You can see for yourself how this can be. A thirty-foot garden hose is very long when it is stretched out, but if you coil it up, you can squeeze it into a very small space—small enough to fit into a human body.

The gateway to the human digestive system is the mouth. The mouth is more than a simple opening. Just inside the lips is a set of *teeth*, half in the upper jaw and half in the lower jaw. A five-year-old child usually has twenty teeth. These are called *milk teeth*. Before he is grown, he will lose every one of these teeth, but new ones will grow in their place. These are the *permanent teeth*, and there will be thirty-two of them all together.

If you look closely at your teeth, you will see that they are not all alike. Some are shaped like chisels, others come to a point, and still others are large and broad.

Adult humans have a set of 32 teeth: 8 cutting incisors, 4 pointed canines, and 8 premolars and 12 molars for heavy chewing. Only part of a tooth can be seen; it also has a large root extending deep into the gums. The tooth is covered on the outside by hard enamel; within are softer layers of dentin and pulp, and a nerve that can transmit the pain of a toothache.

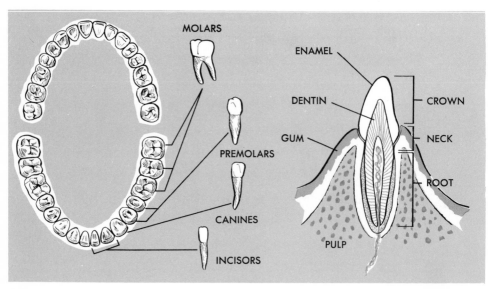

MOLARS

ENAMEL

DENTIN

GUM

PULP

CROWN

NECK

ROOT

PREMOLARS

CANINES

INCISORS

The flat chisel-shaped teeth, which are in the front of your mouth, are called *incisors*. These are the cutting teeth, which you use to bite off pieces of food.

The pointed teeth on each side of the incisors are called *canines*. Our canines merely aid the other teeth. But in carnivores, such as cats and dogs, the canines are longer than the other teeth and help to slash and tear their food. (In fact, the word "canine" comes from a word meaning "dog.")

Beyond the canines are the *premolars* and *molars*, of which there are twenty all together in the adult's set of permanent teeth. These teeth crush and grind our food. Many herbivorous animals, such as horses and cows, have very large and flat molars, which are well suited to grinding the vegetable food they eat. Carnivores, on the other hand, have knife-shaped molars, which help in tearing their food apart. For they generally gulp their food down in chunks rather than grind it into fine bits, as herbivores do.

We can see that our teeth are a sort of combination: we have teeth for cutting and tearing as carnivores do, but we also have teeth for grinding, like the herbivores. This set of teeth helps us in eating many different kinds of foods.

The teeth guard the opening to the *mouth cavity*. This cavity has a curving roof, shaped something like a dome. Attached to the floor of the mouth is the *tongue*. The tongue has many functions. You can find out for yourself one of the most important of these. Hold your tongue tightly down against the floor of your mouth, and try to speak. Your words come out quite blurred, and it is hard for people to understand what you are saying. If you look in the mirror, you will see that even though you are trying to keep your tongue still, it is moving about while you talk and is actually still helping you to form words. A person who had no tongue would not be able to speak understandably.

The tongue is also an important part of the digestive system. If you eat a piece of candy, it tastes sweet to you. If you bite into a dill pickle, it tastes sour. A pretzel tastes salty, and some medicines taste bitter. All these tastes are picked out by special sense cells in your tongue. These special cells are not just scattered over your tongue; they are grouped together in certain places according to the kind of taste. The sense cells of the tongue are found in cup-shaped structures called *taste buds*.

You can make a map of your tongue. First, carefully wipe your tongue dry with a clean piece of cloth or tissue. (If your tongue is wet, moisture may carry the foods you will be testing to all parts of your tongue and confuse the results of the tests.) Now sprinkle a few grains of sugar onto the tip of your tongue. Do you taste anything? Carefully wipe the grains of sugar away, and try the same thing on the sides of your tongue, then the middle, then the back. If your tongue was completely dry, you should not have tasted anything. For the taste buds do not work unless there is moisture about.

Now fill three glasses halfway with water. In one of the glasses, stir in a teaspoonful of sugar. In the second, mix in a teaspoonful of salt. To the third glass add a teaspoonful of vinegar and stir. (Be sure to use a clean spoon for each.) Wrap a bit of cotton around the end of each of three matchsticks. Dip one into the sugar solution, and touch it carefully to the back of your tongue. Now try the sides of your tongue, then the middle, and finally the tip. Where did you taste the sweetness? Sketch a picture of your tongue on a piece of paper, and mark "sweet" in the proper place.

Now rinse and dry your tongue and repeat the tests with the salt solution, and then after rinsing and drying your tongue again, with the vinegar. (Vinegar tastes sour.) When you have finished, check your map of the tongue with the drawing on page 15.

You may notice that you did not test for a bitter taste. None of the common foods you eat has a pure bitter taste. Scientists often use the drug quinine to test for this taste, and in the drawing on page 15 you can see where they have found the "bitter" taste buds to be.

In addition to tasting food, the tongue also helps to move the food around in your mouth as you chew. It shapes the food into a rounded ball called a *bolus* (BOLE-us) and then gives the bolus a final push when you swallow.

Just before it is swallowed, the bolus is pushed back by the tongue into a passageway called the *pharynx* (FAR-inks), which is behind the mouth cavity. The pharynx is also connected to passageways that lead from the nose. And so, air as well as food passes through the pharynx.

Curiously enough, part of what we normally think of as taste is not really taste at all. Part of the "taste" of foods is actually their smell, which is picked up by special sense cells in the nasal passages. You may have noticed that when you have a cold and your nose is stopped up, even your favorite foods seem to be tasteless. You can try an experiment to

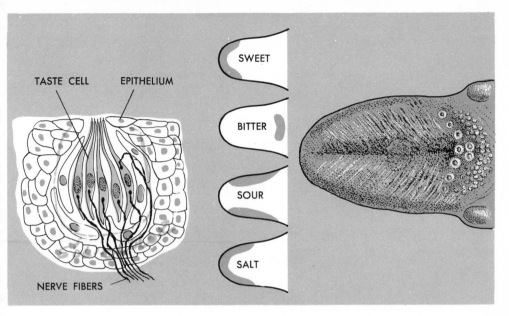

Special taste buds on different parts of the tongue permit us to taste sweet, sour, salty, and bitter foods.

show how important smell is in identifying foods.

Cut small pieces out of an apple, a pear, and a potato, each piece the same size and shape as the others. Rinse your mouth out with water, and carefully dry your tongue. Have a friend blindfold you. Then, while you are holding your nose, have him place one of the three bits of food onto the middle of your tongue. You will find that you can only guess what food it is, for you can neither taste it nor smell it.

Now stop holding your nose. You should now be able to tell easily whether you have a piece of apple, pear, or potato in your mouth, from its smell alone.

(You may have guessed right even with your nose closed. For the tongue has a fine sense of touch and may be able to tell the difference between how pieces of apple, pear, and potato feel.)

The pharynx branches into two passageways. One, an air passage called the *trachea* (TRAY-kee-uh), leads down to the lungs. The other, a food passageway called the *esophagus* (e-SOPH-a-gus), leads down to the stomach. The body has a special device that keeps the food from going down the air passage "by mistake." The opening of the air passage called the *glottis* (GLOT-is), is guarded by a trapdoor called the *epiglottis* (ep-i-GLOT-is). When you swallow, the epiglottis closes fast upon the glottis and keeps the food from entering the trachea.

When you swallow, your epiglottis closes down like a trapdoor to keep food from slipping down into the trachea.

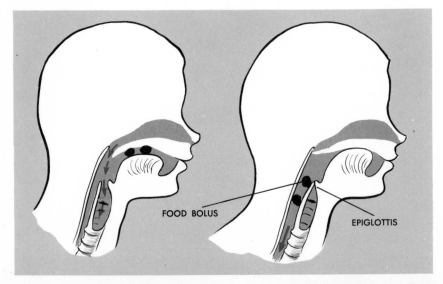

FOOD BOLUS

EPIGLOTTIS

Perhaps your mother has told you never to talk with food in your mouth. This is wise advice. For in addition to being bad manners, talking with food in your mouth can be dangerous. While you talk, the epiglottis opens and closes to let air in and out of your voice box (which sits at the top of the trachea). So if you are talking and trying to swallow food at the same time, it is possible for some food to slip into your air passage. Some people have choked to death in this way.

There is no trapdoor at the top of the esophagus, and so there is nothing to prevent air from being swallowed with the food. A baby often swallows a great deal of air when it drinks its milk. That is why its mother must pat it on the back after a meal, to bring up the bubble of swallowed air in a "burp."

The esophagus is a long muscular tube, which leads directly to the stomach. Before the first astronauts went out into space, scientists were worried about whether they would be able to eat properly. When you eat, gravity helps to carry the food down the esophagus to your stomach. But out in space there is no gravity. Scientists on earth were not quite sure what would happen when an astronaut swallowed.

It turned out that there was no problem at all. For when food is swallowed, waves of contractions

17

in the esophagus naturally push the food along to the stomach. The movement of food toward the stomach will continue in the absence of gravity and even against the force of gravity. Food that you swallow will reach your stomach while you are lying down and even if you are upside down.

Between the esophagus and the stomach there is a different kind of trapdoor. It is a circular muscle called a *sphincter* (SFINK-ter), which closes in some-what like the shutter on a camera. The sphincter muscle at the top of the stomach keeps food and liquids from splashing back into the esophagus. You may have noticed that a young baby frequently "spits up" a mouthful of milk or food. This does not mean that he is sick. It is just that his sphincter muscle does not work perfectly yet, and food is spilling over from his full stomach.

The *stomach* looks like a bag, which can get larger or smaller depending on how much food and liquid are inside it. When the stomach is full, waves of contractions sweep along its muscular walls and churn the food inside. (When the stomach is empty, its walls may also contract. When this happens, you feel hunger pangs.)

Sometimes food does not remain in the stomach, but is vomited out. A special vomiting center in the brain sends out signals that make the walls of the stomach contract and send everything gushing out, up the esophagus. This can happen if you accidentally eat some poison, and so vomiting can help to protect you. (Certain poisons work very well in killing rats because rats are one of the few animals that are not able to vomit.) Vomiting can also occur when you are ill, or when you are seasick or carsick.

In the stomach the food is churned into a soupy mash called *chyme* (KIME). Another sphincter at the bottom of the stomach opens every few minutes, and a small amount of chyme is squirted out into the next part of the digestive tract, the *small intestine*.

The small intestine is by far the longest part of the digestive tract. In a grown man it may be more than twenty feet long. It is coiled around and around and fits neatly into the *abdomen* (AB-doe-men), the part of the body just below the stomach. The first part of the small intestine, which stretches for less than a foot beyond the stomach, is called the *duodenum* (dew-o-DEE-num).

The muscular walls of the small intestine contract in waves to churn the chyme and push it along. It is in the small intestine that most of the nourishing parts of the food are absorbed into the body.

At last the remains of the food—the undigested parts—reach the *large intestine*. A sphincter separates the small and large intestines. Just below the

19

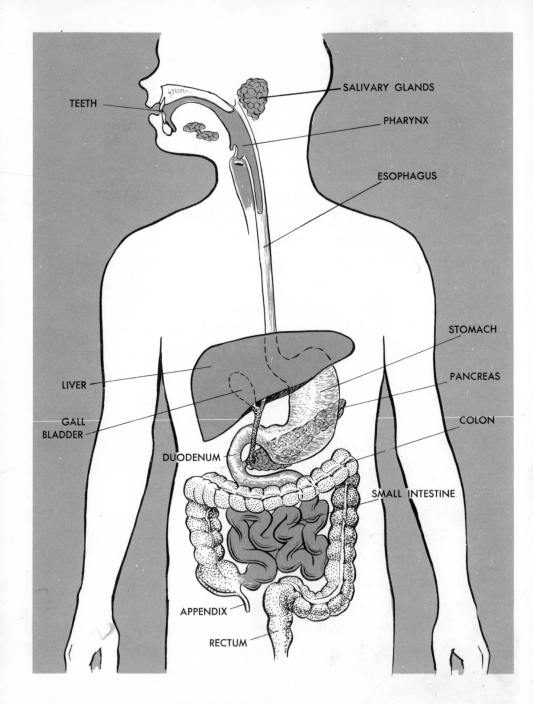

SALIVARY GLANDS

TEETH

PHARYNX

ESOPHAGUS

STOMACH

LIVER

PANCREAS

GALL
BLADDER

COLON

DUODENUM

SMALL INTESTINE

APPENDIX

RECTUM

The human digestive system.

sphincter, the tube of the digestive tract balloons downward into a dead end. This is called the *cecum* (SEE-kum). At the bottom of the cecum is a finger-shaped tube, the *appendix* (ap-PEN-diks). Sometimes the appendix becomes infected. Then it becomes a danger to the rest of the body, for it may swell and finally burst, spreading germs throughout the whole abdomen. When an appendix becomes infected, a condition called *appendicitis* (ap-pen-di-SITE-is), a surgeon must take it out.

From the cecum, the large intestine extends up the right side of the body to the top of the abdomen, then across to the left side, turns down again, and finally loops over to the middle of the body. This curving part of the large intestine is called the *colon* (COLE-on). It passes into a straight tube called the *rectum* (RECK-tum). This final part of the large intestine leads out of the body through an opening called the *anus* (ANE-us).

In the large intestine water is removed from the undigested food matter and it becomes more and more solid. It is stored in the rectum as a solid, brown material called *feces* (FEE-sees). When you move your bowels, the sphincter muscle at the anus opens up, and, with aid of contractions of your abdominal and other muscles, a portion of the feces is forced out.

21

4

How Food Is Used by the Body

What happens to a roast-beef sandwich when you eat it?

Surprisingly, the first steps in digestion begin even before the first bite. When you look at the sandwich and smell the odor of the meat and bread, your mouth begins to water. Three pairs of glands, the *salivary* (SAL-i-vary) *glands*, pour a fluid called *saliva* (sa-LYE-va) into your mouth.

When you bite into the sandwich and chew on a mouthful of meat and bread, your tongue mixes the food thoroughly with saliva. While the food is being moistened and shaped into a bolus, chemical changes are taking place. For the saliva contains substances that are capable of breaking down food products. These substances are called *enzymes* (EN-zimes). They are chemicals that help other chemicals to react easily.

Two enzymes found in saliva are *amylase* (AM-i-lase) and *maltase* (MAUL-tase). These words end with the same syllable, "ase." This is not just a coincidence. The names of nearly all the enzymes end in "ase." The first part of an enzyme's name comes from the chemical on which it works. Most enzymes work on only one chemical or on a small number of similar chemicals. The chemical on which an enzyme works is called its *substrate* (SUB-strate).

The substrate of the enzyme amylase is a substance found in starch. This substrate is called *amylose* (AM-i-lohs). When amylase works on amylose, this starchy substance is broken down to a sugar called *maltose* (MAUL-tohs). Then the enzyme maltase works on maltose and breaks it down to a simpler sugar called *glucose* (GLUE-kohs).

Enzymes digest starches to sugars.

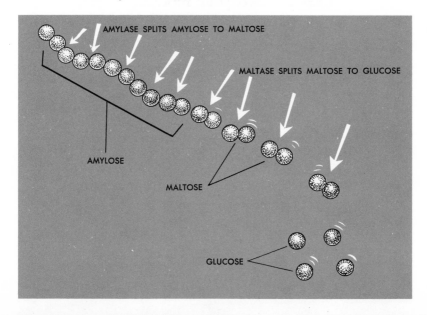

You can see for yourself how the enzymes of the saliva work on food. Take three small glasses, and put about a quarter of an inch of water in each one. Place a drop of iodine in the first glass. A golden brown color spreads through the water.

Now take a small piece of cracker (smaller than a half of a dime), and crumble it into the second glass. (A pinch of cornstarch will do just as well.) Swirl the water about in the glass, and then add a drop of iodine to this glass. In a moment a blue color appears and grows darker, until the tiny cracker bits are a very dark blue. This is a test for starch. Whenever starch is present, iodine will turn it deep blue.

Now wash a rubber band carefully, then place it in your mouth and chew on it for a minute or two. You will soon feel saliva flowing into your mouth. Squirt some of the saliva into the last glass. Add some crumbled cracker, swirl, and add a drop of iodine. The mixture turns dark blue.

Now put all the glasses aside to stand for a while, and look at them every few minutes. The first two glasses stay the same. But the mixture in the third glass gets lighter and lighter until all the blue color disappears. What has happened to the starch? The amylase from your saliva has broken it down into sugar.

As you swallow the bolus, very little of the starch in the bread from your sandwich has been broken down into maltose or glucose. If you had chewed a little longer, more of the starch would have been worked on by the enzymes in your saliva.

The bolus passes down your esophagus, through the sphincter, and into your stomach. Even before the bolus entered your stomach, cells in the lining of the stomach began secreting, or pouring out, chemicals into the stomach. The mixture of these chemicals is known as *gastric juice.* In this gastric juice there is a great deal of a very strong acid called *hydrochloric* (hye-droh-KLOR-ik) *acid.* This acid is so strong that if some of your own gastric juice were poured on your hand it would give you a terrible burn. And yet, it does not harm your stomach at all. It seems amazing, since the lining of your stomach is made of cells far more delicate than the dead cells that are found in the palm of your hand. Your stomach cells are protected by a thin coat of a slimy substance called *mucus* (MEW-kus). You can see how this kind of protection works by smearing a thin coat of Vaseline on a piece of paper. If you drop water on the protected paper, it does not soak in; it just rolls off the coat of greasy Vaseline.

You may have heard of people who have *ulcers*. Doctors are not completely sure how ulcers are formed, but they think that when a person is very nervous for a long time, the cells in his stomach lining do not make enough mucus. As a result, parts of the stomach (and even the duodenum) may not be protected, and the acid eats away some of the stomach cells. Ulcers are the sores that are formed. They can be very painful and even dangerous. A person may lose a great deal of blood from a bleeding ulcer, or the stomach acid may eat all the way through the wall, spilling food and bacteria out into the body cavity.

The gastric juice contains not only hydrochloric acid but also an important enzyme, *pepsin* (PEP-sin). (The name of this enzyme does not end in "ase" because it was discovered before scientists agreed on the rules for naming enzymes.)

Pepsin does not work on starches. It works on a different kind of chemicals called *proteins* (PRO-teens). Starches are made up of long chains of building blocks called sugars. (Remember that maltose and glucose are sugars.) Proteins are also

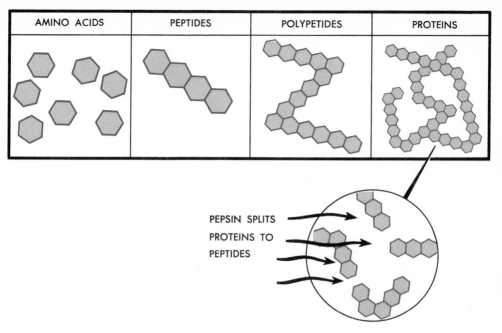

Enzymes digest proteins to peptides and amino acids.

made up of long chains. But their building blocks are chemicals of a different sort, called *amino* (a-MEEN-oh) *acids*. These amino acids can link together to form short chains, called *peptides*, which in turn can link together to form longer chains (polypeptides) or still longer chains (proteins).

Pepsin can break some of the bonds that hold the amino acids of protein chains together. As a result, peptides are formed in the stomach.

The roast-beef sandwich that you began eating at the beginning of the chapter contains a great deal of protein. The roast beef is mostly protein.

The milk and eggs that were used in making the bread contain protein. Even the grain from which the flour was ground contains some protein. All these proteins are worked on by pepsin in the stomach.

Every few minutes some of the peptides formed, along with other materials in the chyme, are squirted through the sphincter at the bottom of the stomach into the small intestine. In this way, the entire stomach is emptied within a few hours after a meal.

Up to this point, only one or two enzymes at a time have been working on the roast-beef sandwich. For when the bolus reached the stomach, the strong acid soon stopped the action of the amylase and maltase from the saliva. But now, in the small intestine, two large groups of enzymes begin to act on the remains of the roast-beef sandwich.

One group of enzymes is secreted by a gland called the *pancreas* (PAN-cree-as). This is a long leaf-shaped organ that lies between the stomach and the duodenum. It secretes a mixture of enzymes called *pancreatic juice* through a short tube into the duodenum.

The pancreas makes four different kinds of enzymes. Some of them, like the pepsin of the stomach, work on proteins, breaking them down into peptides, or further into amino acids. Enzymes that work on proteins and peptides all belong to a group called *proteases* (PROTE-ee-ase-es).

The pancreas also secretes an amylase and a maltase. Like the amylase and maltase of the saliva, these enzymes split starchy substances into maltose and maltose into glucose.

A third type of enzyme secreted by the pancreas is *lipase* (LIP-ase). This enzyme works on fats, which belong to a large group of chemicals that scientists call *lipids*. Lipase breaks fats down into smaller building blocks.

The last kind of enzymes made in the pancreas is the *nucleases* (NEW-clee-ase-es). They break down *nucleic* (new-CLAY-ik) *acids*, chemicals that carry the plans or blueprints for cells and even for the whole body.

Glands in the walls of the intestines secrete very much the same kinds of enzymes as the pancreas. Together these enzymes complete the process of digesting the food materials into smaller bits that the body can take up for its own use.

The amino acids and sugars are in a form that can easily be absorbed by the walls of the intestines.

But the large globs of fat remaining from the roast beef cannot easily be attacked by the lipases in the intestines. The enzymes can digest the fat molecules on the outside of the globs, but there are far more fat molecules inside the globs that never come in contact with them. If the fat globs could be broken down into many smaller globs, then the fat molecules inside could be reached by the lipases.

For example, suppose you had two snowballs as as big as grapefruits. If you broke one of them apart into a hundred little snowballs, and placed the large snowball and the hundred small ones under a hot light, you would find that the little snowballs would melt much more quickly than the large ones. In the small snowballs, far more of the snow was exposed to the heat.

None of the enzymes of the pancreas and intestines can break down the large fat globs; but the *liver*, the largest organ in our body, secretes a mixture of substances that solve the problem. This mixture, a yellow or orange liquid called *bile*, empties into the duodenum. Bile breaks up the fat globs into millions of tiny globules, which are easily attacked by the lipases in the intestines.

The digested food materials are of no value to the body as long as they stay within the digestive tract. In order to be used by the body, they must enter the bloodstream. For this they must first pass through the walls of the intestines.

The walls of the intestines are lined with millions of tiny finger-shaped structures called *villi* (VILL-eye; singular, *villus*). These villi are about one millimeter long—about as long as two of the periods on this page, touching each other. In the middle of each villus is a tube, closed at one end called a *lacteal* (lak-TEEL). The lacteals are part of the lymph system, which empties into the bloodstream. Fatty materials pass into the lacteals within the villi and then into the lymph system and eventually into the bloodstream.

Digested food particles are absorbed into the villi in the lining of the small intestine and pass into the bloodstream and lymph system.

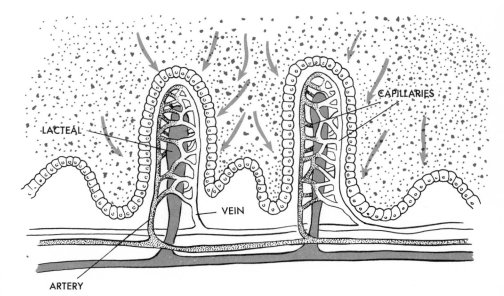

Amino acids and sugars pass into a network of tiny blood vessels that surround the lacteal. They move on into larger and larger blood vessels until they reach the liver. Here they are stored temporarily and then passed on into the bloodstream for further use by the cells of the body.

Sometimes poisons are absorbed into the villi and pass on to the liver. One of the liver's tasks is to change these poisons into other chemicals that will not be harmful to the body.

The whole process in which the food materials pass from the intestines into the blood is called *absorption*. But some of the material that we eat cannot be absorbed at all. *Cellulose* (SELL-yew-lohs) is one of the main materials that the body cannot break down into smaller bits that it can use. Cellulose is the most widespread chemical in the plant world and makes up a large portion of the fruits and vegetables that we eat.

Cellulose and others materials that the body cannot digest pass into the large intestine, along with a great deal of watery material. In this portion of the digestive tract, there is almost no absorption of food, but most of the water is absorbed through the walls of the large intestine. More than twenty-four hours may go by before the remains of the roast-beef sandwich pass out of the body as feces. Along with the undigested food, each day we get rid of billions and billions of bacteria, which make their home in our large intestines. They feed on bits of food that we are unable to use. Some of them can be dangerous, but many, as we shall learn later, are quite helpful.

5

Foods for Living

Think of the people you know. Some are tall and some are short. Some are fat and some are thin. What these people look like depends to some degree on what and how much they eat. If a person eats too much, his body will store the extra food in the form of fat. He could "reduce" by eating less food than his body needs. Then his body would use up some of the stored fats for energy, and he would get thinner.

There are three main types of food substances that the body can use for energy and building materials. These are *carbohydrates* (car-bow-HYE-drates), *fats*, and *proteins*. The starch that you tested for in the cracker and the sugar that you sprinkle on your cereal in the morning are both carbohydrates. The bread in the roast-beef sandwich was also mostly carbohydrate. The slice of roast beef was marbled with bits of white fat. Butter and cooking oil are almost all fat. Milk has some fat in it as well. One of the best sources of proteins is meat, such as the roast beef in the sandwich. Protein is also found in fish, eggs, milk, and many other foods.

In fact, there are very few foods that are *pure* carbohydrate, fat, or protein. Most foods are mixtures of two or even all three of the major food groups.

When it needs energy, the body first calls on carbohydrates. A runner may eat a candy bar just before an important race to give him extra carbohydrates for his body to use for a quick source of

A balanced diet should include foods rich in carbohydrates, fats, and proteins.

CARBOHYDRATES   FATS   PROTEINS

energy. Some of the glucose in the candy bar is absorbed right through the stomach walls into the blood within minutes after the runner eats the candy bar.

There is a certain amount of glucose in our blood at all times. The trillions of cells of the body use this glucose as a source of energy. The amount of glucose in the blood is called the *blood-sugar level*. If this level rises (as it does after a meal), you feel full. If it falls a little, you feel hungry. If it falls too low, the cells of your body will be starved, and you may go into a coma and perhaps even die.

The liver acts as a storehouse for glucose. After a meal, glucose molecules travel to the liver. There they are linked up into long chains to form a sort of animal starch called *glycogen* (GLYE-koe-gen). When the blood-sugar level falls, some of the glycogen in the liver is changed back into glucose and passes into the blood.

Sugars are good food not only for people but also for almost all kinds of creatures, including the bacteria that live in your mouth. If you eat too much candy and other sugary foods, the bacteria in your mouth will multiply rapidly, and you will get more cavities in your teeth.

Scientists can measure the amount of energy released when the body uses foods. They measure this energy in terms of a unit called a *Calorie* (CAL-er-ree). A Calorie is the amount of heat that will raise the temperature of about a quart of water almost 2° Fahrenheit (this is exactly 1° in a different temperature scale that scientists use, called *Centigrade*).

The human body needs a certain amount of energy merely to stay alive. Even if someone stayed in bed for a whole day, his body would use about 1,500 Calories of energy. (This amount is for a man; a child would use much less energy.) But activities such as running, walking, lifting things, and even sitting up or speaking, use up energy. Energy is also used to keep the body warm. The more active a person is, and the colder the weather, the more Calories he will need. A bookkeeper who works at a desk all day may need only about 2,000 Calories a day, while a lumberjack who does heavy work outdoors in very cold weather may need as much as 8,000 Calories a day.

There is more energy per ounce in fats than in either carbohydrates or proteins. As we have seen, digested fats are taken into the body through the lacteals within the villi, pass into the bloodstream, and finally reach the liver. This organ uses the building blocks of fats to make its own types of fatty substances, such as *cholesterol* (koe-LES-ter-ol) and many other kinds. Some of these fatty substances find their way back into the blood and are then stored in special places, called *fat depots*, in various parts of the body. If the body has extra fats to store (they can even be made from excess carbohydrates and proteins), these fats can build up in layers under the skin in nearly all parts of the body. That is how a person gets fat.

Doctors say that Americans eat too much fat. Almost half the Calories of our diet come from fats. With so much fat in our bodies, some of it is laid down on the inside of the walls of our arteries, making the arteries narrower and narrower. As the openings of the arteries get narrower, the heart has to work harder and harder to force enough blood through. Sometimes the narrowed arteries in the heart itself become clogged up, and then the person suffers a heart attack. So doctors are urging Americans to eat less fats and more proteins.

Proteins are the main building materials for the body. There are millions of different kinds of proteins in the living world. Each kind of living thing has its own set of proteins. Cow proteins and chicken proteins are different in many ways from the proteins in our bodies. But even if the proteins in the food we eat were exactly the same as ours, they would have to be digested anyway. For proteins are much too large to pass into the villi in our intestines.

When the amino acids from digested proteins do enter the bloodstream, they are taken up by many cells in the body. There they are turned into parts of the eyes or skin or nerves or muscles. Just about every part of the body has protein in it. Without a good supply of protein in his food each day, a child could not grow properly.

If a person ate a diet containing only pure protein, pure fat, and pure carbohydrate, he would soon die. For our bodies need other things as well. One of the most important of these is water. Humans cannot live for more than a few days without taking in water. You may have read about people fasting for a month or more. But although they may not have eaten any food during this time, they certainly drank some water each day.

Most of the human body (and indeed, the bodies of all living things) is made up of water. If somehow all the water could be taken out of the body of a one-hundred-pound boy, all that would remain

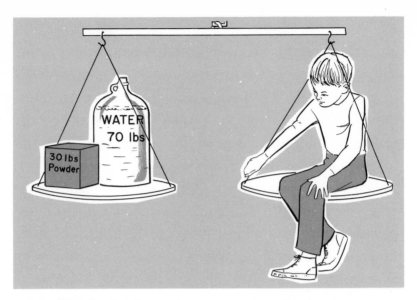

The body tissues are more than half water.

would be a pile of less than thirty pounds of dry powder. Although some of the water within us flows freely as blood, lymph, digestive juices, and other fluids, much of it is bound up with chemicals in the body, such as proteins and carbohydrates. Most of the chemical reactions in the body cannot take place unless water is present. Water is used in the body's heating and cooling systems, and serves many other important functions as well.

The body also needs a number of salts. Common table salt, sodium chloride, is one of these. Salts of magnesium, calcium, potassium, iron, and iodine are only a few of the many other salts that the body must have to live. Many of these salts work with enzymes of the body to help bring about chemical reactions. Some salts or *minerals* are parts of important chemicals in the body. For example, iron is part of the red chemical hemoglobin, which is found in red blood cells and helps to carry oxygen and carbon dioxide through the bloodstream. Iodine is part of a chemical secreted by a gland called the thyroid gland, which helps to tell the cells how fast to use glucose to release energy.

Even a diet containing proteins, carbohydrates, fats, plenty of water, and all the necessary minerals could not keep a person alive and healthy for very long. There is another group of food substances that are necessary for good health and even for life itself. These are the *vitamins* (VITE-a-mins).

Vitamins were not known before the twentieth century. For thousands of years people suffered from *vitamin deficiences* (a lack of vitamins) without realizing what was wrong.

For example, a mysterious disease called *scurvy* (SKUR-vee) used to strike nearly every ship that sailed out on a long voyage. After a while, the crewmen would begin to lose their teeth and bleed easily. Their bones broke easily, and their joints were swollen and painful. Many of them died. No one knew what caused the disease or how to cure it. Not until the eighteenth century was it learned that these sailors were suffering from a lack of something that is found in fresh foods. When this was discovered, a rule was passed stating that all the sailors of the British Navy must eat limes when they sailed on long voyages. (That is how they got their nickname of "Limeys.") Even though there was now a cure for scurvy, it was still not known exactly what substance was lacking in the seamen's usual diet. Finally, in this century, the vital substance was found to be a chemical called *ascorbic* (as-KOR-bik) *acid*, or *vitamin C*. It is found in fresh vegetables and fruits, especially citrus fruits, such as oranges, limes, and grapefruits.

Vitamin C was not the first vitamin discovered. In 1913 an American biochemist, Elmer McCollum, discovered a chemical in fats, which was essential for life. This chemical was named *vitamin A*, and it was decided to call another important chemical, which had been isolated two years earlier, *vitamin B*. (It was the discoverer of vitamin B, Casimir Funk, who first proposed the term "vitamine," which was later changed to "vitamin.") Other vitamins were found, and they were named vitamins C, D, E, etc. However, it was later discovered that vitamin B is actually a mixture of a number of different vitamins found together in such foods as yeast and the outer hulls of cereal grains. When these mixtures were separated, the single vitamins were given such names as vitamin B_1, riboflavin, niacin, vitamin B_6, and vitamin B_{12}.

Milk and fish oils are rich in vitamin A. This vitamin helps to keep the skin and the linings of the respiratory and digestive tracts soft and firm and so helps to provide protection from harmful bacteria. It also helps us to see well at night.

Vitamin D is also found in fish oils and milk. (Manufacturers also add extra vitamin D to milk.)

A good diet should include plenty of vitamins.

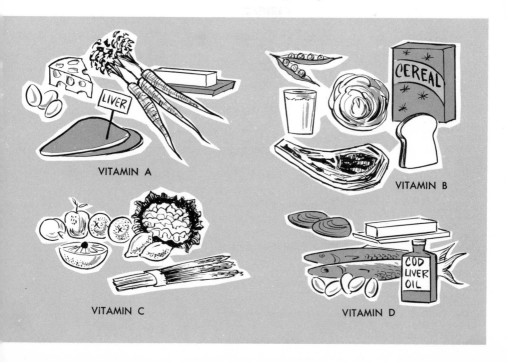

VITAMIN A

VITAMIN B

VITAMIN C

VITAMIN D

Our own bodies can make vitamin D when our bare skin is exposed to the sun. The extra vitamin D that is made in our skin during the summer months is stored in the liver. This vitamin is necessary to keep our bones strong. A child who does not get enough vitamin D while he is growing may have soft bones that bend out of shape and so may be crippled for the rest of his life. This condition is known as *rickets* (RICK-ets).

We can see that vitamins A and D are very important for our health. But too much of these vitamins can be harmful. For the body needs only a certain amount of them and stores any excess in the liver. When the level of either of these two vitamins gets too high, it can be poisonous to the body.

The B vitamins do many different tasks in the body and are found in a great many foods, such as whole-grain cereals, nuts, and liver. A lack of one of the B vitamins, vitamin B_1—which is also called *thiamine* (THYE-a-min)—causes a disease called *beriberi* (berry-BERRY). In this disease, the nerves and muscles start to break down, and eventually the person becomes paralyzed.

A Dutch physician, Christiaan Eijkman (IKE-mahn), was sent to the Dutch East Indies in the late nineteenth century to try to find the cause and cure of beriberi. For a long time, Eijkman tried in vain to find the germ that he thought must be causing the disease. He discovered the real cause quite by accident. One day he noticed that some of the chickens that were being used at the hospital for experiments were sick. They seemed to have beriberi. He tried all sorts of treatments, but nothing helped. Then, suddenly, they all got better. Eijkman soon learned that there was a new cook at the hospital. The old cook had run out of chicken feed and had been feeding the chickens with the same fine white polished rice that was used to feed the human patients. The new cook did not think this was proper and went back to using chicken feed, which was whole rice grains. (The outer hulls were carefully removed from the polished rice that people ate.)

Eijkman found that if he fed the chickens polished rice, they developed beriberi, but then if he fed them whole rice, soon they were well again. When he gave his human patients whole rice, they too recovered from beriberi.

There are more than a dozen different B vitamins. A lack of any one of them causes its own kind of illness.

In addition to the B vitamins, other vitamins are known, such as *vitamin K*, which helps our blood to clot, preventing us from bleeding to death when we get cut. People who do not get enough vitamin K in their diet still may not have a deficiency. Some of the bacteria that live in our large intestine make extra vitamin K, which our bodies can absorb. Bacteria in our intestines also make some B vitamins.

Doctors often prescribe vitamin pills for growing children and for pregnant women. They want to make sure that children will get enough vitamins and minerals to help them grow properly, even if

The seven basic food groups for good health.

they do not always eat enough of the right kinds of foods.

Doctors advise us to eat a *balanced diet*. By this they mean that we must be sure to eat foods that contain proteins, carbohydrates, fats, water, minerals, and vitamins. In the United States today most children are eating a much better balanced diet than their grandparents did. One result of this is that young people today are growing taller than the Americans of fifty years ago.

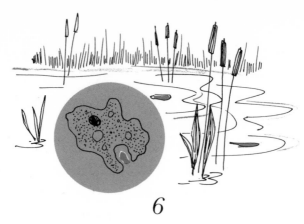

6

Digestion in Lower Animals

In puddles, ponds, lakes, streams, and oceans, countless numbers of tiny creatures are stalking and eating one another. Amebas, which look like colorless globs of jelly, ooze along. If an ameba meets a smaller creature, such as a slipper-shaped paramecium, bulges grow mysteriously out of the ameba's body. Larger and larger they grow, until they are like arms, reaching out to encircle the ameba's prey. The bulges, called *pseudopods* (SUE-do-pods), meet and merge, and soon the prey is trapped within the ameba's own body.

The helpless prey is now imprisoned in a tiny bubble inside the ameba's body. This bubble is called a *food vacuole* (VAK-yew-ole), and the struggling creature within it will soon become the ameba's next meal. Digestive enzymes begin to flow into the food vacuole. These enzymes kill the captured prey and begin to break down its body into simpler materials that the ameba can use. The digested food is gradually absorbed into the parts of the ameba's body that surround the food vacuole. When only indigestible bits of food remain, the vacuole gradually moves through the ameba's body to the outer surface. There it opens up, allowing the waste materials to drift away through the water in which the ameba lives.

Digestion in two one-celled organisms, the ameba and paramecium.

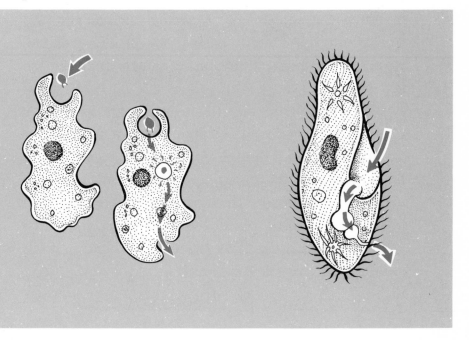

Paramecia digest their food in much the same way that amebas do. But they catch their food in a quite different way. The paramecium has a mouth, leading into a *gullet* (GULL-it), which is something like our throat. Around the gullet are many tiny hairlike structures called *cilia* (SILL-ee-uh). These beat back and forth in rhythm and make currents in the nearby water. Tiny bacteria and single-celled plants in the water are drawn into the paramecium's gullet by the currents.

Unlike our throat, the paramecium's gullet does not lead to a stomach. At the end of the gullet, a food vacuole is formed. Then the food is digested in much the same way as in the ameba. But the waste material always passes out of the paramecium's body in the same place, which is known as the *anal pore*.

Both the ameba and the paramecium are made up of only a single cell. A sponge has a body made up of many cells (though not nearly as many as the trillions of cells that make up our bodies). The bath and kitchen sponges that you may have used are probably made of plastic. But perhaps you have seen a real sponge. It is the dried skeleton of an animal that lives in the sea.

The body of a sponge has thousands of branching channels that open into the water in which it lives. Each of these channels is lined with long whiplike structures called *flagella* (fla-JELL-uh), which beat back and forth to create feeding currents in the water, much like the currents created by the cilia of the paramecium. Minute water creatures and bits of dead matter are carried into the channels, where they become stuck in the tiny branches. They are picked up by wandering cells called *amebocytes* (a-MEE-bow-sites). These cells surround bits of the sponge's food just as amebas catch their prey. The sponge's food is digested in food vacuoles in the amebocytes and stored there until it is needed by the other cells of the sponge's body.

The hydra, a small water-dwelling animal, has a more complicated body than the sponge. It spends most of its time with one end of its long body anchored to the bottom of the pond or a stone or leaf. At the other end of its body is a round mouth, surrounded by a number of waving tentacles. These tentacles are equipped with a varied set of weapons, such as stingers and sticky threads, which can be shot out to catch and paralyze the hydra's prey— other small creatures of the pond.

When a small animal is snared, the hydra's other tentacles wrap around it and draw it into the mouth. After the prey is swallowed, it drops into a digestive cavity, in which proteases break it down into smaller bits. These partly digested bits are taken in by cells in the walls of the cavity, which can send out pseudopods like those of the ameba. Digestion is finished inside food vacuoles within these ameba-like cells. The undigested materials pass back into the digestive cavity, and then, with a mighty contraction of its body, the hydra spits them out through its mouth into the water of the pond.

Digestion in the sponge, hydra, and flatworm.

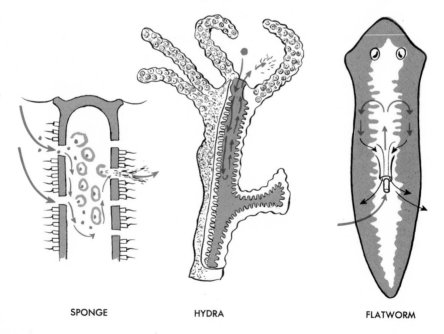

SPONGE   HYDRA   FLATWORM

In the hydra's ocean relative, the jellyfish, digestion takes place in much the same way—partly in a digestive cavity and partly inside food vacuoles within special digesting cells. Scientists have special names for these two types of digestion. Digestion that takes place inside a digestive cavity is called *extracellular digestion*, which means "digestion outside the cells." For even though you might think of the digestive cavity as being inside the hydra's or jellyfish's body, it is actually outside the body cells. Digestion that takes place within cells is called *intracellular digestion*, which means "digestion inside the cells."

In the flatworms that live in ponds and streams, digestion is rather like that in the hydra and its relatives. The flatworm has a mouth and a pharynx in the middle of the underside of its body. It swallows its prey into its pharynx, where the food is broken down into smaller bits that are captured by ameba-like cells. There digestion is finished, and waste products flow back out through the flatworm's mouth.

In more complicated animals, from earthworms up to man, digestion is mainly extracellular. It takes place in a digestive tract, which is a tube that runs through the body.

7

From Worms to Man

The lowly earthworm has more in common with a man than you might think. It has muscles and nerves and blood vessels. Its body is covered with a sort of skin, and inside, running through the length of its body, is a digestive tract—a long tube with a mouth at one end and an anus at the other.

If you look at the diagram of an earthworm, you can see that it looks rather like a tube with a thick wall. The wall is the body of the earthworm, and the inner part of the tube is its digestive tract. This same basic pattern is repeated in more than a million different kinds of animals, including man himself.

There are some important advantages to this kind of digestive system. It permits "one-way traffic" for food. The food enters at one end and passes down the digestive tract until the undigested materials pass out the other end. At a series of "service stations" along the tract, special organs work on the food, gradually breaking it down into usable bits. This can be done much more efficiently than if the undigested food had to go back again the same way, as it does in the hydra and flatworm. With a one-way digestive system an animal can eat a new meal before it has finished digesting its last one.

There is something rather odd in the way the earthworm gets its food. It actually eats its way through the soil. As the worm burrows through the earth, soil is swallowed into its mouth and passes down its digestive tract. There bits of food, such as seeds, pieces of leaves, insect eggs, and tiny soil animals, are digested and absorbed. Waste products from the worm's body are added to the remains of the soil, which passes out of its anus in the form of long tubular *castings*.

Earthworms help to make soil richer and better for growing plants. Their constant burrowing loosens the soil and allows air to get to the plant roots, and the waste products in their castings contain nourishing substances that the plants can take in and use.

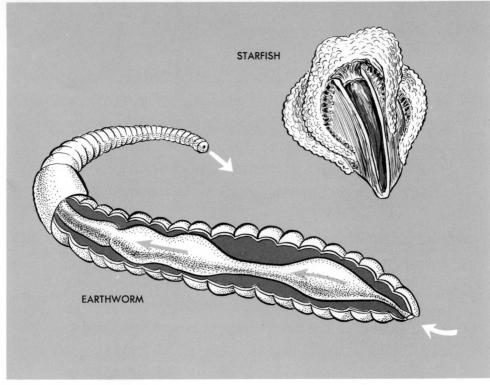

STARFISH

EARTHWORM

The earthworm eats its way through the soil, while the starfish digests its meal outside its body.

A curious variation of digestion is found in starfish. These animals, which live in the sea, have a flattened star-shaped body, with a mouth on the underside and an anus on top. Starfish feed mainly on oysters, clams, and other shelled creatures. When an oyster is caught by a starfish, the oyster clamps its two shells tightly shut. It can hold its shells closed so firmly that a man would find it difficult to pry them apart.

56

The starfish grasps the oyster's shells with rows of small suckers on the undersides of its arms. It holds the shells tightly and slowly pulls outward. At last the oyster tires, and allows its shells to open slightly. The opening may be only a thin crack, but the starfish is ready, and it does a curious thing. It turns its stomach inside out, pushes it out through its mouth, and slides it through the crack between the shells of the oyster! There, within the oyster's shells, digestive juices flow from the stomach of the starfish and partly digest the soft body of its prey. Then the starfish draws its stomach back into its body, sucks in the partly digested bits of its oyster dinner, and finishes its meal.

In many animals, including man, digestion begins with a mechanical process in which food is chopped or ground into smaller pieces. Then follows a chemical process in which enzymes work on the food bits and break them down into molecules that the body can use. In humans and many other animals, the mechanical part of digestion is started off by chewing the food with teeth. Insects do not have teeth like ours, but some of them do have hard mouth parts with which they can chew their food. In addition, they can "chew" their food some more *after* they swallow it.

A grasshopper, for example, bites off pieces of plant leaves and swallows them. The food passes down an esophagus to a chamber called a *crop*, where it is stored for a while. Then it passes into a *gizzard* (GIZZ-erd), where hard plates grind it up into fine pieces. Only then does the food pass into the grasshopper's stomach, where digestive enzymes work on it.

Some insects do not need to chew their food, because they eat only liquid food. Mosquitoes and other insects that bite animals and suck their blood have special mouth parts shaped like a hypodermic needle. They pierce the skin and draw in the liquid like sucking soda up through a straw. Aphids, which

Digestion in the grasshopper and bird.

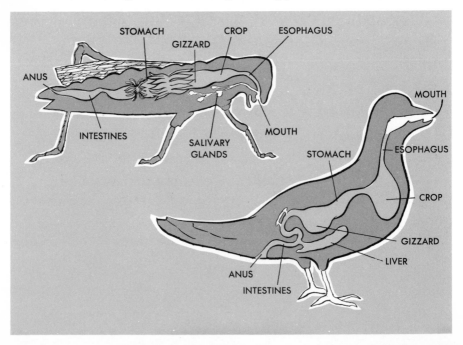

suck plant juices, also have mouth parts that are good for piercing through the plant stems and leaves.

Birds do not have teeth. They may be able to bite off chunks of food with their bills, but they swallow them whole. In a part of the bird's stomach, called the gizzard, strong muscles contract and grind up the food. The grinding is helped by stones, which the birds swallow. If you have ever had a pet parakeet, you may know that it must have not only enough food and water but also small pebbles or gravel to swallow. Without these small stones, it could not digest its food properly.

Special problems of getting and digesting food have been solved by some strange partnerships in the animal world. For example, did you know that termites, insects that have earned a very bad reputation from their practice of eating the wooden frames of people's houses, cannot digest the cellulose in wood at all? Yet wood is made up mostly of cellulose. This substance is digested for termites by tiny one-celled animals that live in their intestines. In much the same way, cows are able to get enough nourishment from a diet of grass only because bacteria living in their digestive tracts break down the cellulose of the plant cells for them.

8

How Plants Use Food

We have said that plants do not eat as animals do. Instead they make their own food from simple chemicals that they take in from the air and soil. *Chlorophyll* (CLORE-o-fill), the green coloring material in plants, makes this possible. With the help of chlorophyll, plant cells use the energy from sunlight to form sugars from water and a gas called *carbon dioxide*. This process is known as *photosynthesis* (foe-toe-SIN-theh-sis). It is one of the most important processes that take place on our planet earth. All the energy that we get from the foods we eat and all the energy that our machines use when they burn oil or gas or coal can be traced back to energy from sunlight, stored by plants in products of photosynthesis.

Although plants make their own food, they do need to take in many substances from the world around them. First of all, they need plenty of water. Just like our cells, plant cells are made up mostly of water. They use water for photosynthesis and in their various chemical reactions. Water keeps plant cells firm and plump and actually helps to hold the plants up. It seems strange to think of a

How water is used by the plant: 1) water takes part in photosynthesis and other chemical reactions; 2) water evaporates from the leaves; 3) water helps to hold plant cells firm; 4) water is absorbed through tiny root hairs; 5) water is transported through the plant in thin tubes.

plant having a water "skeleton," but you may have noticed that a rubber hot-water bag is flabby and limp when it is empty but solid and firm when it is filled with water. The water in plant cells works in a similar way. In addition to the water that is used by plants in these ways, an enormous amount of water escapes into the air through the leaves of plants. A single corn plant loses more than fifty *gallons* of water during the growing season, and a tree may lose that much in just one day. If this water is not replaced, the plant will wilt and die. Plants take in water mainly through their roots.

Along with the water, plants take in many mineral salts. For plants need minerals, just as we do. They get their minerals from the soil or water in which they live. But plants cannot use all the minerals in the ground. Some minerals remain tightly bound to the soil. Plants can use only the ones that dissolve in water.

When crops have been planted in the same field year after year, the plants gradually take the minerals out of the soil. If they are not replaced, the soil becomes so poor that plants cannot grow properly on it. There are a number of things that a good farmer can do to keep his fields rich and fertile.

He can put back minerals by adding fertilizers, such as manure, ground bones, and chemicals manufactured in large fertilizer factories. He can also rotate his crops. This means that one season he plants a crop that takes minerals out of the soil. Then the next season he plants a different crop that makes extra amounts of certain chemicals and actually puts minerals back into the soil. Some of these crops are the *legumes* (LEG-yumes), a family of plants that includes peas and beans. These plants make the soil richer in nitrogen.

All plants need nitrogen. But they cannot use the gas nitrogen that makes up about four fifths of the air that we breathe. The nitrogen that plants can use must be bound up into salts called *nitrates* (NITE-rates). There are some microscopic creatures in the soil that bind nitrogen from the air into salts. But legumes have their own bacteria that makes nitrates for them. These bacteria live in little round swellings, called *nodules* (NODE-yules), on the roots of the legumes. The partnership between the bacteria and the legumes works in much the same way as that between the termites and the microscopic animals that live in their intestines. The bacteria find shelter in the nodules of the

The nodules on the roots of the peanut plant contain nitrogen-fixing bacteria, which bind nitrogen from the air into nitrates.

legumes, and they make substances that the plants can use. Extra nitrates pass out into the soil and can be used by later crops grown there.

The sugars that plants make in photosynthesis can be used for energy or built up into more complicated building materials for the plants. The foods that plants make may not all be used right away. Large amounts of food may be stored in the form of starch in the roots, stems, or fruits of the plants. Some vegetables that we eat, such as carrots

and turnips, are plant roots. Others, such as potatoes and asparagus stalks, are parts of plant stems.
Bananas, apples, and peaches are all fruits, while
peas and corn are seeds. All of them contain large
amounts of stored starch.

During the night, and at other times when photosynthesis cannot be carried on, plants may use their
stored food. To do this they must digest it, just as
animals do. This digestion takes place inside the
plant cells, for they do not have any special digestive systems as we do. But many of the chemical
reactions of digestion are basically the same as
those in animals. Amylases break starches down
into sugars, and proteins and fats may also be
broken down by digestive enzymes.

9

The Hungry World

In the American supermarket, shelves are filled with "diet foods." Advertisements on radio and television and in magazines and newspapers constantly advise us on how to get thin. Many Americans have a serious problem: they are overweight.

It seems almost unbelievable that in this same world, millions of people are starving to death.

Doctors have found that if a child does not get enough protein while he is young, his body will not grow properly, and he may waste away and die. Even if he lives, his brain may not develop as it should, and he will not be as bright as he could have been. Once he grows up, this can never be corrected, no matter how well he eats. This disease is called *kwashiorkor* (kwash-ee-OR-kor). The name comes from African words meaning "a disease that a child gets when the next baby is born." For when a new baby is born, a small child can no longer drink his mother's milk, and the food that he eats often does not contain enough protein, or the right kind of protein.

We know that proteins are made up of building blocks called amino acids. There are about twenty different amino acids found in our bodies. Our cells can make twelve of them from other chemicals. But the other eight must be taken in with our food. These are called *essential amino acids* because we must have them in our diet in order to live and grow.

Animal proteins contain all the essential amino acids. But meats are the most expensive foods of all, and many people in the world are so poor that they cannot afford to have meat very often. Potatoes, corn, and cereal grains, such as rice, wheat, barley, and oats, are much cheaper and make up most of the diet of people in poorer lands. Although these foods consist mainly of starch, they do contain some proteins. But their proteins do not have enough of all the essential amino acids. Corn, for example, has enough of only six of the essential amino acids. It has only very small amounts of an amino acid called *tryptophan* (TRIP-toe-fane) and of another essential amino acid called *lysine* (LYE-seen). Scientists have recently developed new types of corn that do have enough lysine and tryptophan to provide for good health.

Scientists are also working on improving the food qualities of other crops. New varieties of rice and wheat grow much faster and give a higher yield than the old ones.

Improving crops and methods of growing them is only part of the answer. We need new sources of food. One of these lies in the sea. Oceans cover more than two thirds of our planet. And yet less than 2 percent of the food eaten by the people of the world comes from the seas. Some scientists believe that the great farms of the future will be sea farms, yielding great harvests of fish and other sea life.

Many of the fish that swarm in the oceans are not usually considered good to eat. But even these fish can be turned into nourishing food by drying them and grinding them into fish flour. This powder does not have any "fishy" odor or taste at all, and it can be mixed with other foods to make protein-rich dishes. A fish-flour meal might cost only a

Food for the future.

penny, and there are enough fish in the sea to provide food for the whole world.

Scientists are looking everywhere for new sources of food. Even grass and the leaves from bushes and trees have been turned into good sources of protein. The process is not being used yet to feed the hungry millions because it is still too expensive.

One of the most promising new "crops" may be tiny creatures, each so small that it could not be seen without a microscope. It seems unbelievable that such minute creatures as yeast and bacteria could be used to supply food for people. Yet these small organisms can multiply in fantastic numbers and can grow on very cheap raw materials, such as crude petroleum (the oil from which gasoline is made). Less than 3 percent of the oil produced each year could be used to grow bacteria and yeast that would give us more protein than all the animal protein produced each year in the whole world. In the future, instead of buying a hamburger, you may find yourself asking for a yeastburger.

In these and many other ways, scientists are learning how to produce enough food so that the people of the future need never go hungry.

Index

gastric juice, 25–26
gizzard, 58–59
glottis, 16
glucose, 23, 36
glycogen, 36
grasshopper, 58
gullet, 50

heart disease, 38
herbivorous animals, 7, 11
horses, 11
hydra, 51–53
hydrochloric acid, 25

incisors, 11
intracellular digestion, 53, 65
iodine, 40–41
iodine test for starch, 24
iron, 40–41

jellyfish, 53

kwashiorkor, 66–67

lacteal, 31–37
large intestine, 19, 21, 32–33
legumes, 63
lions, 7
lipase, 29–30
lipids, 29

liver, 30, 32, 36, 38
lymph system, 31
lysine, 68

maltase, 23, 29
maltose, 23, 29
mice, 7
minerals, 41, 47, 62–63
molars, 11
mosquito, 58
mouth, 9
mouth cavity, 12
mucus, 25

nitrates, 63
nitrogen, 63
nodules, 63
nucleases, 29
nucleic acids, 29

omnivorous animals, 8
oyster, 56–57

pancreas, 28–29
pancreatic juice, 28
paramecium, 50
pepsin, 26–28
peptides, 27–29
pharynx, 14
photosynthesis, 60–61, 64–65